foreword

Nuts are great for snacking and are a delicious addition to baked goods, from cookies or bars to decadent desserts. Although they are not usually the main component of a recipe, nuts are perfect for highlighting other flavours, taking things up a notch and giving many recipes that special finishing touch.

Nuts are also nutritional powerhouses; they are high in antioxidants, which protect the body against cell-damage, and also help keep your heart healthy. So toss a few into your favourite recipe and indulge away!

We've chosen recipes from our library to represent your favourite nuts— and although we know that peanuts are technically legumes, we couldn't resist including them (along with peanut butter too!). Go nuts and engage all your senses with this collection of recipes from Company's Coming!

Jean Paré

rich chocolate brownies

A surprise ingredient—tofu—provides these brownies with added nutrition. Soy milk can also be substituted to make them dairy-free.

Granulated sugar	2 cups	500 mL
All-purpose flour	1 cup	250 mL
Chopped pecans	1 cup	250 mL
Semi-sweet chocolate chips	1 cup	250 mL
Cocoa, sifted if lumpy	1/2 cup	125 mL
Package of silken tofu (12 1/4 oz., 349 g), drained	1/2	1/2
Cooking oil	1/4 cup	60 mL
Large eggs	3	3
CHOCOLATE ICING		
Icing (confectioner's) sugar	1 cup	250 mL
Cocoa, sifted if lumpy	1/4 cup	60 mL
Silken tofu	3 tbsp.	45 mL
Milk	1 1/2 tsp.	7 mL
Chopped pecans	3 tbsp.	45 mL

Combine first 5 ingredients in large bowl.

Process next 3 ingredients in blender until smooth. Add to flour mixture. Mix well. Pour into greased foil-lined 9 x 13 inch (23 x 33 cm) pan. Bake in 350°F (175°C) oven for about 35 minutes until set. Brownies will still be soft inside. Let stand in pan on wire rack until cool. Chill, covered, for 2 to 3 hours until firm. Remove from pan.

Chocolate Icing: Beat first 4 ingredients in small bowl until smooth. Spread over brownies.

Sprinkle with pecans. Cuts into 32 pieces.

1 piece: 170 Calories; 7 g Total Fat (3 g Mono, 1.5 g Poly, 2 g Sat); 15 mg Cholesterol; 25 g Carbohydrate; 2 g Fibre; 3 g Protein; 10 mg Sodium

chewy slice

Enjoy the classic combination of walnuts and coconut in a simple square.

FIRST LAYER

All-purpose flour	1 1/2 cups	375 mL
Brown sugar, packed	1/2 cup	125 mL
Cold butter (or hard margarine)	1/3 cup	75 mL

SECOND LAYER

Large eggs	2	2
Brown sugar, packed	1 cup	250 mL
Vanilla extract	1 tsp.	5 mL
Salt	1/4 tsp.	1 mL
Chopped walnuts	1 cup	250 mL
Crisp rice cereal	1 cup	250 mL
Medium unsweetened coconut	1 cup	250 mL

First Layer: Combine flour and sugar in medium bowl. Cut in butter until mixture resembles coarse crumbs. Press firmly into ungreased 9 x 9 inch (23 x 23 cm) pan. Bake in 350°F (175°C) oven for 15 minutes.

Second Layer: Beat eggs in large bowl until frothy. Add next 3 ingredients. Beat until smooth.

Add remaining 3 ingredients. Mix well. Spoon over first layer. Bake for 25 minutes. Let stand in pan on wire rack until cool. Cuts into 36 squares.

1 square: 110 Calories; 6 g Total Fat (1 g Mono, 1.5 g Poly, 3 g Sat); 10 mg Cholesterol; 15 g Carbohydrate; trace Fibre; 2 g Protein; 45 mg Sodium

fruit and nut loaf

Do you go nuts for candied fruit and almonds? This pretty, light-coloured loaf has everything you're looking for!

Butter (or hard margarine), softened	1/2 cup	125 mL
Granulated sugar	1 cup	250 mL
Large eggs	2	2
Milk	1 cup	250 mL
Vanilla extract	1 tsp.	5 mL
Almond extract	1/2 tsp.	2 mL
All-purpose flour	2 1/8 cups	530 mL
Chopped mixed glazed fruit	3/4 cup	175 mL
Raisins (or currants)	3/4 cup	175 mL
Chopped almonds	1/2 cup	125 mL
Baking powder	2 tsp.	10 mL
Salt	1/2 tsp.	2 mL

Cream butter and sugar in medium bowl. Add eggs, 1 at a time, beating well after each addition.

Add next 3 ingredients. Stir.

Combine remaining 6 ingredients in large bowl. Add butter mixture. Stir until just moistened. Spread in greased 9 x 5 x 3 inch (23 x 12.5 x 7.5 cm) loaf pan. Bake in 350°F (175°C) oven for about 1 hour until wooden pick inserted in centre comes out clean. Let stand in pan for 10 minutes before removing to wire rack to cool. Cuts into 16 slices.

1 slice: 245 Calories; 8.7 g Total Fat (3.2 g Mono, 0.9 g Poly, 4.1 g Sat); 39 mg Cholesterol; 39 g Carbohydrate; 1 g Fibre; 4 g Protein; 172 mg Sodium

chocolate panforte

A traditional Italian dessert, panforte (pronounced pan-FOHR-tay) is rich with chocolate and festive fruit.

Raw cashews, toasted (see Tip, page 64)	1 2/3 cups	400 mL
All-purpose flour	1 1/2 cups	375 mL
Whole natural almonds, toasted (see Tip, page 64)	1 1/2 cups	375 mL
Chopped dried apricot	1/2 cup	125 mL
Rings of glazed pineapple, chopped	4	4
Chopped red glazed cherries	1/4 cup	60 mL
Cocoa, sifted if lumpy	1/4 cup	60 mL
Cut mixed peel	1/4 cup	60 mL
Ground cinnamon	2 tsp.	10 mL
Granulated sugar	1 cup	250 mL
Liquid honey	1 cup	250 mL
Semi-sweet chocolate baking squares (1 oz., 28 g, each), chopped	4	4

Combine first 9 ingredients in extra-large bowl.

Combine sugar and honey in small saucepan. Heat and stir on medium until sugar is dissolved. Bring to a boil on medium-high. Boil for 5 minutes without stirring. Remove from heat. Add to nut mixture. Stir well.

Heat and stir chocolate in small heavy saucepan on lowest heat until almost melted. Remove from heat. Stir until smooth. Add to nut mixture. Stir. Press evenly in bottom of greased parchment paper-lined 9 x 13 inch (23 x 33 cm) pan. Bake in 375°F (190°C) oven for 20 minutes. Let stand in pan on wire rack until cooled completely. Invert onto work surface. Remove parchment paper. Cut in half lengthwise. Cut each half crosswise into 1/2 inch (12 mm) slices. Makes 48 bars.

1 bar: 138 Calories; 4.9 g Total Fat (3 g Mono, 0.9 g Poly, 0.7 g Sat); 0 mg Cholesterol; 23 g Carbohydrate; 1 g Fibre; 2 g Protein; 2 mg Sodium

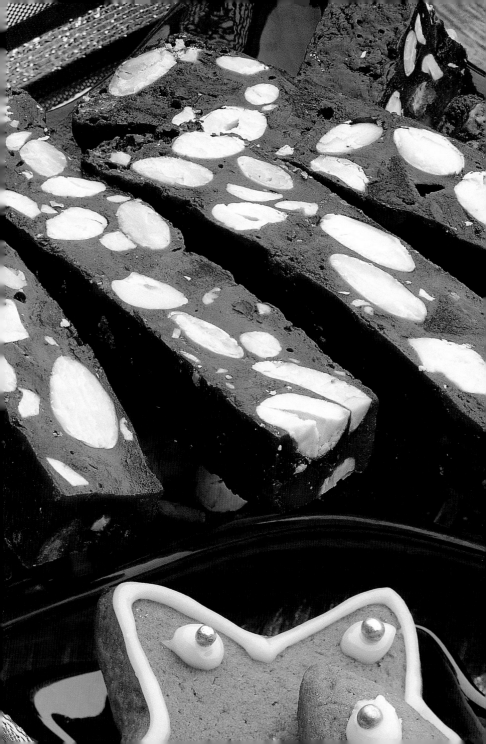

maple nut fingers

These tasty "fingers" are filled with three kinds of nuts and infused with maple flavour.

All-purpose flour	1 1/2 cups	375 mL
Icing (confectioner's) sugar	1/4 cup	60 mL
Baking powder	1/2 tsp.	2 mL
Ground cinnamon	1/4 tsp.	1 mL
Ground nutmeg	1/4 tsp.	1 mL
Salt	1/4 tsp.	1 mL
Cold butter (or hard margarine), cut up	1/2 cup	125 mL
Large egg, fork-beaten	1	1
Coarsely chopped pecans	3/4 cup	175 mL
Coarsely chopped raw macadamia nuts	3/4 cup	175 mL
Coarsely chopped sliced almonds	1/2 cup	125 mL
Brown sugar, packed	1/2 cup	125 mL
Butter (or hard margarine), melted	1/2 cup	125 mL
Golden corn syrup, warmed	1/2 cup	125 mL
All-purpose flour	1/4 cup	60 mL
Large egg, fork-beaten	1	1
Maple extract	1/2 tsp.	2 mL

Line greased 9 x 13 inch (23 x 33 cm) pan with parchment (not waxed) paper, leaving 1 inch (2.5 cm) overhang on both long sides. Combine first 6 ingredients in large bowl. Cut in butter until mixture resembles coarse crumbs.

Add egg. Stir well. Press evenly in bottom of prepared pan. Bake on centre rack in 350°F (175°C) oven for about 15 minutes until golden brown.

Sprinkle next 3 ingredients over top.

Beat remaining 6 ingredients in small bowl. Pour over nuts. Bake in 350°F (175°C) oven for about 15 minutes until topping is golden brown and set. Let stand in pan on wire rack until cool. Remove from pan. Cut crosswise into 16 narrow strips. Cut each strip into 3 fingers. Makes 48 fingers.

1 finger: 115 Calories; 8 g Total Fat (3.9 g Mono, 0.7 g Poly, 3 g Sat); 20 mg Cholesterol; 10 g Carbohydrate; 1 g Fibre; 1 g Protein; 66 mg Sodium

christmas fudge

Festive fudge for the holidays. This can be made ahead and frozen, or kept in the refrigerator.

Granulated sugar	3 cups	750 mL
Half-and-half cream	3/4 cup	175 mL
Corn syrup	3 tbsp.	45 mL
Butter	1 tbsp.	15 mL
Almond extract	1 tsp.	5 mL
Vanilla extract	1 tsp.	5 mL
Chopped pecans	1/2 cup	125 mL
Sliced Brazil nuts	1/2 cup	125 mL
Chopped glazed pineapple	1/3 cup	75 mL
Chopped green glazed cherries	1/4 cup	60 mL
Chopped red glazed cherries	1/4 cup	60 mL

Combine first 4 ingredients in large heavy saucepan. Bring to a boil on medium-low, stirring often. Heat and stir until mixture reaches soft ball stage (about 234°F, 112°C) on candy thermometer or until small amount dropped into very cold water forms a soft ball that flattens on its own accord when removed. Remove from heat. Let stand for about 10 minutes until crust forms on top but liquid is still warm. Beat until slightly thickened and a little lighter in colour.

Add almond and vanilla extracts. Beat with spoon until it loses its shine.

Quickly stir in remaining 5 ingredients. Press with greased hands into greased 8 x 8 inch (20 x 20 cm) pan. Let stand until cool. Cuts into 36 pieces. Makes about 2 1/2 pounds (1.1 kg) fudge.

1 piece: 120 Calories; 3 g Total Fat (1 g Mono, 0.5 g Poly, 1 g Sat); trace Cholesterol; 22 g Carbohydrate; 0 g Fibre; trace Protein; 10 mg Sodium

rum balls

Customize these rum balls with whatever coating strikes your fancy!

Semi-sweet chocolate chips	1 cup	250 mL
Sour cream	1/2 cup	125 mL
Graham cracker (or vanilla wafer) crumbs	3 cups	750 mL
Icing (confectioner's) sugar	1/2 cup	125 mL
Corn syrup	2 tbsp.	30 mL
Rum extract	2 tbsp.	30 mL
Finely chopped pecans (or walnuts)	1 cup	250 mL

Coatings (such as granulated sugar, cocoa, ground hazelnuts, ground walnuts, chocolate sprinkles or ground pecans)

Heat chocolate chips and sour cream in heavy saucepan on lowest heat, stirring constantly, until chocolate is almost melted. Do not overheat. Remove from heat. Stir until smooth.

Add next 5 ingredients. Mix well. Roll into 1 inch (2.5 cm) balls.

Roll balls in your choice of coatings. Store in airtight container. Chill. Makes about 78 balls.

1 ball (without coatings): 45 Calories; 2.5 g Total Fat (0.5 g Mono, 0 g Poly, 1 g Sat); 0 mg Cholesterol; 6 g Carbohydrate; trace Fibre; trace Protein; 30 mg Sodium

blondie brownies

Blondes have more fun, you know—especially when treats like this can be made with just four ingredients!

Biscuit mix	2 cups	500 mL
Brown sugar, packed	1 1/2 cups	375 mL
Large eggs	3	3
Chopped pecans	1 cup	250 mL

Beat first 3 ingredients in large bowl for about 3 minutes until smooth.

Add pecans. Stir. Spread evenly in greased 9 x 9 inch (23 x 23 cm) pan. Bake in 350°F (175°C) oven for about 30 minutes until wooden pick inserted in centre comes out clean. Let stand in pan on wire rack for 10 minutes. Cuts into 36 squares.

1 square: 117 Calories; 5.0 g Total Fat (2.5 g Mono, 1.0 g Poly, 1.0 g Sat); 16 mg Cholesterol; 17 g Carbohydrate; 1 g Fibre; 2 g Protein; 148 mg Sodium

almond ginger triangles

Crystallized ginger adds something special to these tantalizing treats.

Butter (or hard margarine)	1/2 cup	125 mL
Finely crushed vanilla wafers (about 54 wafers)	2 cups	500 mL
Butter (or hard margarine), softened	3/4 cup	175 mL
Granulated sugar	3/4 cup	175 mL
Vanilla extract	1 tsp.	5 mL
Large eggs	3	3
Ground almonds	1 1/2 cups	375 mL
Minced crystallized ginger	1/4 cup	60 mL
All-purpose flour	3 tbsp.	45 mL
Semi-sweet chocolate baking squares (1 oz., 28 g, each), grated	2	2
Ground nutmeg	1/4 tsp.	1 mL
Salt	1/4 tsp.	1 mL
Sliced blanched almonds	1/3 cup	75 mL

Icing (confectioner's) sugar, for dusting

Melt first amount of butter in medium saucepan. Remove from heat.
Add wafer crumbs. Mix well. Press firmly into greased 9 x 13 inch
(22 x 33 cm) pan.

Beat second amount of butter and sugar in medium bowl until light
and fluffy. Add vanilla. Stir. Add eggs, 1 at a time, beating well after
each addition.

Add next 6 ingredients. Stir. Spread evenly over crust.

Sprinkle with sliced almonds. Bake in 350°F (175°C) oven for about
35 minutes until wooden pick inserted in centre comes out clean. Let
stand in pan on wire rack until cool. Cut into 20 rectangles. Cut each in
half diagonally, for a total of 40 triangles.

Dust with icing sugar. Makes 40 triangles.

*1 triangle: 126 Calories; 9.4 g Total Fat (3.5 g Mono, 0.8 g Poly, 4.5 g Sat);
35 mg Cholesterol; 10 g Carbohydrate; trace Fibre; 2 g Protein; 96 mg Sodium*

chocolate pecan balls

These no-bake balls can also be made as drop cookies.

Granulated sugar	2 cups	500 mL
Butter (or hard margarine)	1/2 cup	125 mL
Milk	1/2 cup	125 mL
Quick-cooking rolled oats	2 cups	500 mL
Chopped pecans (or walnuts), toasted (see Tip, page 64)	1 cup	250 mL
Cocoa, sifted if lumpy	1/2 cup	125 mL
Vanilla extract	1 tsp.	5 mL
Finely chopped pecans (or walnuts), toasted (see Tip, page 64)	1 cup	250 mL

Combine first 3 ingredients in large saucepan. Bring to a boil on medium, stirring often. Boil gently for 3 minutes. Remove from heat.

Add next 4 ingredients. Stir well. Let stand until cool enough to handle. Shape into 1 inch (2.5 cm) balls.

Roll balls in second amount of pecans. Store in airtight container. Makes 36 balls.

1 ball: 130 Calories; 7 g Total Fat (3.5 g Mono, 1.5 g Poly, 2 g Sat); 5 mg Cholesterol; 16 g Carbohydrate; 1 g Fibre; 2 g Protein; 20 mg Sodium

pistachio shortbread

Very attractive and not too sweet. Look for shelled pistachios in the Asian section of the grocery store or at East Indian grocery stores.

Butter, softened	1 cup	250 mL
Granulated sugar	2/3 cup	150 mL
Almond extract	1/2 tsp.	2 mL
Drops of green food colouring (optional)	3 – 4	3 – 4
All-purpose flour	2 1/4 cups	550 mL
Pistachios, finely chopped	1/2 cup	125 mL
Ground cardamom	1/2 tsp.	2 mL
Pistachios, finely chopped	1/2 cup	125 mL

Beat butter and sugar in large bowl until light and fluffy.

Add extract and food coloring. Stir.

Add next 3 ingredients. Mix well. Dough will be dry and crumbly. Knead until no dry flour remains. Divide dough into 2 equal portions. Roll into 1 1/2 inch (3.8 cm) diameter logs.

Sprinkle second amount of pistachios over 12 x 12 inch (30 x 30 cm) sheet of waxed paper. Roll dough in pistachios to coat completely. Wrap in plastic wrap. Chill for several hours or overnight. Cut into 1/4 inch (6 mm) slices. Arrange about 1 inch (2.5 cm) apart on ungreased cookie sheets. Bake in 325°F (160°C) oven for about 15 minutes until edges are golden. Let stand on cookie sheets for 5 minutes before removing to wire racks to cool. Makes about 84 cookies.

1 cookie: 45 Calories; 3 g Total Fat (1 g Mono, 0 g Poly, 1.5 g Sat); 5 mg Cholesterol; 5 g Carbohydrate; 0 g Fibre; trace Protein; 15 mg Sodium

chocolate hazelnut cookies

These appealing cookies are rich with chocolate chunks. Each cookie is topped with hazelnuts and a white chocolate drizzle.

Butter (or hard margarine)	1/2 cup	125 mL
Semi-sweet chocolate baking squares (1 oz., 28 g, each), chopped	1 1/2	1 1/2
All-purpose flour	1 1/4 cups	300 mL
Brown sugar, packed	3/4 cup	175 mL
Large eggs, fork-beaten	2	2
Cocoa, sifted if lumpy	2 1/2 tbsp.	37 mL
Coarsely chopped hazelnuts (filberts), toasted (see Tip, page 64) and skins removed (see Tip, page 64)	3/4 cup	175 mL
Milk chocolate chips	1/2 cup	125 mL
White chocolate baking squares (1 oz., 28 g, each), chopped	2	2
Hazelnuts (filberts)	42	42
White chocolate baking squares (1 oz., 28 g, each), chopped	2	2

Heat butter and semi-sweet chocolate in large heavy saucepan on lowest heat, stirring constantly, until almost melted. Remove from heat. Stir until smooth.

Add next 4 ingredients. Stir until combined. Add next 3 ingredients. Mix well. Drop, using 1 tbsp. (15 mL) for each, about 2 inches (5 cm) apart onto greased cookie sheets. Place 1 hazelnut on top of each mound. Bake in 350ºF (175ºC) oven for 8 to 10 minutes until just firm. Let stand on cookie sheets for 5 minutes before removing to wire racks to cool.

Heat second amount of white chocolate in heavy saucepan on lowest heat, stirring constantly, until almost melted. Remove from heat. Stir until smooth. Spoon into resealable freezer bag with tiny piece snipped off 1 corner. Drizzle over cookies. Let stand until set. Makes about 42 cookies.

1 cookie: 105 Calories; 6.4 g Total Fat (3.7 g Mono, 0.5 g Poly, 1.8 g Sat); 11 mg Cholesterol; 11 g Carbohydrate; 1 g Fibre; 2 g Protein; 36 mg Sodium

raisin pecan squares

Simple to make, and simply delicious!

Pecan pieces, toasted (see Tip, page 64)	1 1/2 cups	375 mL
Golden raisins	1 1/4 cups	300 mL
Medium unsweetened coconut	1 cup	250 mL
Milk chocolate chips	1 cup	250 mL
Can of sweetened condensed milk	11 oz.	300 mL

Combine first 4 ingredients in medium bowl. Spread evenly in greased foil-lined 9 x 13 inch (23 x 33 cm) pan.

Drizzle condensed milk evenly over pecan mixture. Do not stir. Bake in 375ºF (190ºC) oven for about 15 minutes until bubbling. Reduce heat to 350ºF (175ºC). Bake for another 10 to 12 minutes until golden. Let stand until cool. Cuts into 24 squares.

1 square: 188 Calories; 11.1 g Total Fat (4.3 g Mono, 1.4 g Poly, 4.9 g Sat); 7 mg Cholesterol; 22 g Carbohydrate; 1 g Fibre; 3 g Protein; 29 mg Sodium

chocolate almond fudge

Dark chocolate and toasted almonds—what could be better?

Miniature marshmallows	9 cups	2.25 L
Granulated sugar	2 cups	500 mL
Evaporated milk	2/3 cup	150 mL
Butter (or hard margarine)	1/2 cup	125 mL
Salt, pinch		
Dark chocolate bars (3 1/2 oz., 100 g, each), chopped	3	3
Almond extract	1 tsp.	5 mL
Slivered almonds, toasted (see Tip, page 64)	2 1/2 cups	625 mL

Line 9 x 9 inch (23 x 23 cm) pan with foil, leaving 1 inch (2.5 cm) overhang on 2 sides. Grease foil with cooking spray. Combine first 5 ingredients in large heavy saucepan. Heat and stir on medium until mixture comes to hard boil. Boil for 5 minutes, stirring constantly. Remove from heat.

Add chocolate and extract. Stir until smooth.

Add almonds. Mix well. Spread evenly in prepared pan. Chill for about 3 hours until firm. Holding foil, remove from pan. Cuts into 64 pieces.

1 piece: 118 Calories; 5.9 g Total Fat (3.3 g Mono, 0.8 g Poly, 1.5 g Sat); 1 mg Cholesterol; 16 g Carbohydrate; 1 g Fibre; 2 g Protein; 25 mg Sodium

salty sweet peanut chews

These sweet and salty treats are ideal for snack attacks of any sort.

Butter (or hard margarine), softened	1/2 cup	125 mL
Smooth peanut butter	1/2 cup	125 mL
Brown sugar, packed	1 cup	250 mL
Large egg	1	1
All-purpose flour	1 cup	250 mL
Baking powder	1/2 tsp.	2 mL
Baking soda	1/4 tsp.	1 mL
Salt, sprinkle		
Miniature marshmallows	3 cups	750 mL
Peanut butter chips	1 cup	250 mL
Golden corn syrup	2/3 cup	150 mL
Butter (or hard margarine)	1/4 cup	60 mL
Vanilla extract	2 tsp.	10 mL
Coarsely chopped salted peanuts	2 cups	500 mL
Crisp rice cereal	2 cups	500 mL

Line 9 x 13 inch (23 x 33 cm) pan with foil, leaving 1 inch (2.5 cm) overhang on 2 sides. Grease foil with cooking spray. Beat first 3 ingredients in large bowl until light and fluffy. Add egg. Beat well.

Combine next 4 ingredients in small bowl. Add to peanut butter mixture. Mix until no dry flour remains. Spread mixture evenly in prepared pan. Bake in 350°F (175°C) oven for about 15 minutes until edges are golden.

Sprinkle with marshmallows. Bake for about 2 minutes until marshmallows start to puff. Let stand in pan on wire rack for 10 minutes.

Heat and stir next 4 ingredients in large saucepan on medium until smooth.

Add peanuts and cereal. Stir well. Immediately spread evenly over marshmallows. Chill for about 1 hour until firm. Holding foil, remove from pan. Cuts into 40 squares.

1 square: 186 Calories; 10.4 g Total Fat (5.3 g Mono, 2 g Poly, 2.4 g Sat); 6 mg Cholesterol; 22 g Carbohydrate; 1 g Fibre; 4 g Protein; 168 mg Sodium

breakfast bars

Wrap and freeze these bars individually for grab-and-go snacks.

Water	2 cups	500 mL
Large eggs	2	2
Package of blueberry bran muffin mix	2 lbs.	900 g
Chopped pecans, toasted (see Tip, page 64)	1 cup	250 mL
Chopped pitted dates	1 cup	250 mL

Beat water and eggs in large bowl until well combined. Add muffin mix. Stir until smooth.

Add pecans and dates. Stir well. Spread evenly in greased 9 x 13 inch (23 x 33 cm) pan. Bake in 350°F (175°C) oven for about 40 minutes until wooden pick inserted in centre comes out clean. Cuts into 24 bars.

1 bar: 203 Calories; 8.1 g Total Fat (4.1 g Mono, 2.5 g Poly, 1 g Sat); 18 mg Cholesterol; 30 g Carbohydrate; 1 g Fibre; 3 g Protein; 211 mg Sodium

noodle power

Tasty little stacks that will disappear fast.

Butterscotch chips	1 cup	250 mL
Semi-sweet chocolate chips	1 cup	250 mL
Butter (or hard margarine)	1/4 cup	60 mL
Smooth peanut butter	1/4 cup	60 mL
Dry chow mein noodles	2 cups	500 mL
Unsalted peanuts	1 cup	250 mL

Heat first 4 ingredients in large heavy saucepan on lowest heat, stirring often, until chips are almost melted. Do not overheat. Remove from heat. Stir until smooth.

Add noodles and peanuts. Stir until coated. Mixture will be soft. Drop, using 2 tsp. (10 mL) for each, onto waxed paper-lined cookie sheets. Let stand until set. May be chilled to speed setting. Makes about 30 cookies.

1 cookie: 123 Calories; 8.3 g Total Fat (3.7 g Mono, 1.9 g Poly, 2.2 g Sat); 0 mg Cholesterol; 12 g Carbohydrate; 1 g Fibre; 2 g Protein; 47 mg Sodium

caramel nut squares

These squares contain pecans in both the chewy base and the sticky-sweet topping.

BOTTOM LAYER

All-purpose flour	1 cup	250 mL
Finely chopped pecans	1 cup	250 mL
Quick-cooking rolled oats	3/4 cup	175 mL
Brown sugar, packed	2/3 cup	150 mL
Baking powder	1/2 tsp.	2 mL
Salt	1/2 tsp.	2 mL
Cold butter (or hard margarine), cut up	1/2 cup	125 mL
Large egg, fork-beaten	1	1

TOP LAYER

Miniature marshmallows	3 cups	750 mL
Caramel ice cream topping	2/3 cup	150 mL
Chopped pecans	1 1/3 cups	325 mL

Bottom Layer: Combine first 6 ingredients in large bowl.

Cut in butter until mixture resembles coarse crumbs. Add egg. Stir well. Press evenly in bottom of greased 9 x 13 inch (23 x 33 cm) pan. Bake in 350°F (175°C) oven for 10 minutes.

Top Layer: Sprinkle marshmallows over hot crust. Drizzle ice cream topping over marshmallows. Sprinkle with second amount of pecans. Bake for about 25 minutes until golden brown. Let stand in pan on wire rack until cooled completely. Cut with hot, wet knife to prevent sticking. Cuts into 54 squares.

1 square: 122 Calories; 7 g Total Fat (3.5 g Mono, 1.2 g Poly, 1.8 g Sat); 11 mg Cholesterol; 15 g Carbohydrate; 1 g Fibre; 1 g Protein; 79 mg Sodium

cracker crunch

A graham cracker treat that will please kids and adults alike.

Whole graham crackers	30	30
Butter	1 cup	250 mL
Brown sugar, packed	1 cup	250 mL
Sliced (or chopped) almonds (or walnuts or pecans)	1 cup	250 mL
Ground cinnamon, sprinkle (optional)		
Semi-sweet chocolate chips	3/4 cup	175 mL

Line greased 10 x 15 inch (25 x 38 cm) jelly roll pan with graham crackers, trimming to fit if necessary.

Combine butter and brown sugar in medium saucepan. Heat and stir on medium until starting to boil. Boil gently for 3 minutes, without stirring. Pour evenly over graham crackers.

Sprinkle with almonds and cinnamon. Bake in 350°F (175°C) oven for about 8 minutes until bubbling and edges are slightly browned.

Sprinkle with chocolate chips. Let stand in pan on wire rack until cool. Cuts into 30 pieces.

1 piece: 140 Calories; 10 g Total Fat (3 g Mono, 0.5 g Poly, 5 g Sat); 15 mg Cholesterol; 14 g Carbohydrate; trace Fibre; 1 g Protein; 65 mg Sodium

nutty biscotti

Chock full of nuts—perfect to serve with coffee or a glass of milk. For a special touch, try dipping one end of each biscotti into melted chocolate.

Butter (or hard margarine), softened	1/4 cup	60 mL
Granulated sugar	3/4 cup	175 mL
Large eggs	2	2
Egg white (large)	1	1
Vanilla extract	1 tsp.	5 mL
Hazelnut liqueur (optional)	1 tbsp.	15 mL
All-purpose flour	2 1/2 cups	625 mL
Baking soda	1 tsp.	5 mL
Salt	1/4 tsp.	1 mL
Flaked hazelnuts (filberts), toasted (see Tip, page 64)	2/3 cup	150 mL

Beat butter and sugar in large bowl until light and fluffy.

Add next 4 ingredients. Beat well.

Add remaining 4 ingredients. Mix well. Turn out onto lightly floured surface. Knead 6 times. Place on greased baking sheet. Shape into 16 inch (40 cm) long log. Bake in 350°F (175°C) oven for 30 minutes. Remove from oven. Let stand on baking sheet for about 20 minutes until cool enough to handle. Using serrated knife, cut log diagonally into 1/2 inch (12 mm) slices. Arrange on same baking sheet. Bake in 275°F (140°C) oven for 12 minutes. Turn slices over. Turn oven off. Let stand in oven for about 30 minutes until dry and crisp. Makes about 24 biscotti.

1 biscotti: 110 Calories; 4.5 g Total Fat (2 g Mono, 0 g Poly, 1.5 g Sat); 15 mg Cholesterol; 17 g Carbohydrate; trace Fibre; 2 g Protein; 95 mg Sodium

chocolate almond cookies

Switch up the chocolate in these big, chewy cookies to suit your taste. Will it be milk, dark or white chocolate—or how about all three?

Butter, softened	1 1/2 cups	375 mL
Brown sugar, packed	2 cups	500 mL
Granulated sugar	1 cup	250 mL
Large eggs	4	4
Almond extract	2 tbsp.	30 mL
All-purpose flour	4 2/3 cups	1.15 L
Baking soda	2 tsp.	10 mL
Salt	2 tsp.	10 mL
Milk (or dark or white) chocolate bars (3 1/2 oz., 100 g, each), coarsely chopped	6	6
Slivered almonds, toasted (see Tip, page 64)	1 cup	250 mL

Beat butter and both sugars in large bowl until light and fluffy. Add eggs, 1 at a time, beating well after each addition. Add extract. Beat until smooth.

Combine next 3 ingredients in medium bowl. Add to butter mixture. Mix until no dry flour remains.

Add chocolate and almonds. Stir. Drop, using 3 tbsp. (50 mL) for each, about 3 inches (7.5 cm) apart onto greased cookie sheets. Bake in 350°F (175°C) oven for about 11 minutes until edges turn golden. Do not overbake. Cookies may still look slightly undercooked in centre. Let stand on cookie sheets for 5 minutes before removing to wire racks to cool. Makes about 32 cookies.

1 cookie: 350 Calories; 16 g Total Fat (6 g Mono, 1 g Poly, 8 g Sat); 45 mg Cholesterol; 45 g Carbohydrate; 2 g Fibre; 5 g Protein; 310 mg Sodium

hazelnut shortbread

A delicious, nutty twist on traditional shortbread cookies.

Butter (or hard margarine), softened	1 cup	250 mL
Granulated sugar	1 cup	250 mL
Hazelnuts, toasted (see Tip, page 64), skins removed (see Tip, page 64), and finely chopped	1 cup	250 mL
All-purpose flour	2 cups	500 mL
Baking powder	1/4 tsp.	1 mL
Salt	1/4 tsp.	1 mL
Egg white (large), fork-beaten	1	1
Sanding (decorating) sugar	2 tbsp.	30 mL

Beat butter and sugar in large bowl until light and creamy. Add hazelnuts. Stir.

Combine next 3 ingredients in medium bowl. Add to butter mixture. Stir until soft, crumbly dough forms. Shape into flattened disc. Roll out dough between 2 sheets of lightly floured waxed paper to about 1/3 inch (8 mm) thickness. Remove top sheet of waxed paper. Cut out dough using lightly floured 2 inch (5 cm) round fluted cookie cutter. Roll out scraps to cut more rounds. Arrange, about 1 inch (2.5 cm) apart, on ungreased cookie sheets.

Brush with egg white. Sprinkle with sanding sugar. Bake in 375°F (190°C) oven for about 7 minutes until edges start to turn golden. Let stand on cookie sheets for 5 minutes before removing to wire racks to cool. Cool cookie sheets between batches. Makes about 42 cookies.

1 cookie: 104 Calories; 6.4 g Total Fat (2.7 g Mono, 0.4 g Poly, 3 g Sat); 12 mg Cholesterol; 10 g Carbohydrate; trace Fibre; 1 g Protein; 64 mg Sodium

sour cream nut rolls

Always a favourite—the sour cream filling makes these special.

Ground almonds	2 1/2 cups	625 mL
Granulated sugar	1/2 cup	125 mL
Milk	1/4 cup	60 mL
Almond extract	1 tsp.	5 mL
Cold butter (or hard margarine)	1 cup	250 mL
All-purpose flour	2 cups	500 mL
Egg yolks (large)	2	2
Sour cream	1/2 cup	125 mL

Combine first 4 ingredients in medium bowl.

Cut butter into flour in large bowl until mixture resembles fine crumbs.

Whisk egg yolks and sour cream in small bowl until well combined. Slowly add to flour mixture, stirring with fork until mixture starts to come together. Do not overmix. Divide dough into 2 equal portions. Shape each portion into 6 inch (15 cm) long log. Flatten slightly. Roll out 1 log on lightly floured surface to 12 x 16 inch (30 x 40 cm) rectangle. Cut into 2 inch (5 cm) squares. Spoon about 1 tsp. (5 mL) almond mixture along centre of each square. Fold opposite corners diagonally over filling. Pinch together to seal. Arrange about 2 inches (5 cm) apart on ungreased cookie sheets. Bake in 350ºF (175ºC) oven for 10 to 12 minutes until golden. Let stand on cookie sheets for 5 minutes before removing to wire racks to cool. Repeat with remaining log and almond mixture. Makes about 96 rolls.

1 roll: 46 Calories; 3.3 g Total Fat (2 g Mono, 0.4 g Poly, 0.7 g Sat); 5 mg Cholesterol; 4 g Carbohydrate; trace Fibre; 1 g Protein; 25 mg Sodium

christmas cookies

Celebrate the season with the classic festive pairing of fruit and nuts.

Butter (or hard margarine), softened	1 cup	250 mL
Brown sugar, packed	3/4 cup	175 mL
Large egg	1	1
All-purpose flour	1 1/4 cups	300 mL
Baking soda	1/2 tsp.	2 mL
Ground cinnamon	1/2 tsp.	2 mL
Salt	1/2 tsp.	2 mL
Chopped walnuts	1 cup	250 mL
Chopped Brazil nuts	1/2 cup	125 mL
Slivered almonds	1/2 cup	125 mL
Chopped pitted dates	1/2 cup	125 mL
Chopped glazed cherries	1/2 cup	125 mL
Glazed pineapple slices, chopped	2	2

Beat butter and brown sugar in large bowl until light and fluffy. Add egg. Beat well.

Combine next 4 ingredients in medium bowl. Add to butter mixture. Mix until no dry flour remains.

Add remaining 6 ingredients. Mix well. Drop, using 1 1/2 tbsp. (25 mL) for each, about 2 inches (5 cm) apart onto greased cookie sheets. Bake in 350ºF (175ºC) oven for 10 to 12 minutes until golden. Let stand on cookie sheets for 5 minutes before removing to wire racks to cool. Makes about 48 cookies.

1 cookie: 112 Calories; 7.5 g Total Fat (3.9 g Mono, 2 g Poly, 1.3 g Sat); 4 mg Cholesterol; 10 g Carbohydrate; 1 g Fibre; 2 g Protein; 88 mg Sodium

pecan balls

*Dress up your cookie platter! These are also known as Mexican Wedding
Cakes or Russian Tea Cakes.*

Butter (or hard margarine), softened	1 cup	250 mL
Icing (confectioner's) sugar	1/2 cup	125 mL
Vanilla extract	2 tsp.	10 mL
All-purpose flour	2 1/4 cups	550 mL
Ground pecans	1 cup	250 mL
Icing (confectioner's) sugar, approximately	1/2 cup	125 mL

Beat first 3 ingredients in large bowl until smooth.

Add flour in 2 additions, mixing well after each addition, until no dry flour
remains. Add pecans. Mix well. Roll into 1 inch (2.5 cm) balls. Arrange
about 2 inches (5 cm) apart on ungreased cookie sheets. Bake in 325ºF
(160ºC) oven for about 20 minutes until golden. Let stand on cookie sheets
for about 5 minutes until cool enough to handle.

Roll each ball in second amount of icing sugar in small bowl until coated.
Place on waxed paper-lined cookie sheets. Let stand until cool. Makes
about 66 balls.

*1 ball: 61 Calories; 4 g Total Fat (2.6 g Mono, 0.6 g Poly, 0.7 g Sat); 0 mg Cholesterol;
6 g Carbohydrate; trace Fibre; 1 g Protein; 34 mg Sodium*

back to square one

Sweet, peanutty squares with a smooth chocolate topping.

Brown sugar, packed	1/2 cup	125 mL
Corn syrup	1/2 cup	125 mL
Smooth peanut butter	1/2 cup	125 mL
Butter (or hard margarine)	6 tbsp.	90 mL
Crisp rice cereal	2 cups	500 mL
Finely chopped unsalted peanuts	1 cup	250 mL
Semi-sweet chocolate chips	1 cup	250 mL
Smooth peanut butter	1/3 cup	75 mL

Combine first 4 ingredients in large saucepan. Heat and stir on medium until smooth. Remove from heat.

Add cereal and peanuts. Stir well. Press firmly into greased 9 x 9 inch (23 x 23 cm) pan.

Heat chocolate chips and second amount of peanut butter in small heavy saucepan on lowest heat, stirring constantly, until almost melted. Remove from heat. Stir until smooth. Spread over cereal mixture. Chill. Cuts into 36 squares.

1 square: 140 Calories; 9 g Total Fat (1.5 g Mono, 0.5 g Poly, 3.5 g Sat); 5 mg Cholesterol; 14 g Carbohydrate; 1 g Fibre; 3 g Protein; 65 mg Sodium

macadamia nut brownies

Make these brownies for the macadamia lovers in your life.

Brown sugar, packed	1 3/4 cups	425 mL
Butter (or hard margarine), cut up	1/2 cup	125 mL
Semi-sweet chocolate baking squares (1 oz., 28 g, each), cut up	4	4
Large eggs, fork-beaten	2	2
All-purpose flour	1 cup	250 mL
Baking powder	1/4 tsp.	1 mL
Salt	1/4 tsp.	1 mL
Macadamia nuts, toasted (see Tip, page 64) and coarsely chopped	3/4 cup	175 mL

Heat and stir first 3 ingredients in heavy medium saucepan on medium-low until smooth. Remove from heat. Let stand until cool.

Add eggs. Stir.

Add remaining 4 ingredients. Stir until well combined. Spread evenly in greased 9 x 9 inch (23 x 23 cm) pan. Bake in 350°F (175°C) oven for about 30 minutes until just set. Let stand in pan on wire rack until cool. Cut into 16 squares. Cut each square in half diagonally. Makes 32 triangles.

1 triangle: 130 Calories; 6.4 g Total Fat (4 g Mono, 0.4 g Poly, 1.7 g Sat); 13 mg Cholesterol; 18 g Carbohydrate; 1 g Fibre; 1 g Protein; 66 mg Sodium

hit-the-trail bars

Homemade granola bars always trump store-bought—especially when they're this easy to make.

Quick-cooking rolled oats	4 cups	1 L
Coarsely chopped whole (or sliced) natural almonds	2 cups	500 mL
Can of sweetened condensed milk	11 oz.	300 mL
Butter (or hard margarine), melted	1/2 cup	125 mL

Combine rolled oats and almonds in large bowl.

Add condensed milk and butter. Mix well. Spread evenly in well-greased 10 x 15 inch (25 x 38 cm) jelly roll pan. Bake in 325°F (160°C) oven for about 25 minutes until golden. Let stand on wire rack for 10 minutes. Cut into bars while still warm. Makes 16 bars.

1 bar: 333 Calories; 18.9 g Total Fat (10.9 g Mono, 3.2 g Poly, 3.7 g Sat); 8 mg Cholesterol; 34 g Carbohydrate; 4 g Fibre; 9 g Protein; 104 mg Sodium

walnut ginger crisps

These elegant appetizers are perfect to serve with sweet or savoury offerings—they're equally delicious with ice cream or as part of a cheese platter.

All-purpose flour	1 cup	250 mL
Minced crystallized ginger	1/3 cup	75 mL
Ground cardamom	1/2 tsp.	2 mL
Egg whites (large), room temperature	3	3
Brown sugar, packed	1/3 cup	75 mL
Walnut halves	1 1/4 cups	300 mL

Combine first 3 ingredients in small bowl.

Beat egg whites and brown sugar in medium bowl until stiff peaks form. Fold in flour mixture until no dry flour remains.

Fold in walnuts. Spread evenly in greased parchment paper-lined 9 x 5 x 3 inch (23 x 12.5 x 7.5 cm) loaf pan. Bake in 350°F (175°C) oven for about 25 minutes until golden and firm. Let stand in pan on wire rack for 45 minutes. Remove loaf from pan. Using serrated knife, cut into 1/8 inch (3 mm) slices. Arrange on ungreased baking sheet. Bake in 300°F (150°C) oven for about 15 minutes, turning at halftime, until dry and crisp. Let stand on baking sheet on wire rack until cool. Makes about 36 crisps.

1 crisp: 50 Calories; 2.3 g Total Fat (0.3 g Mono, 1.6 g Poly, 0.2 g Sat); 0 mg Cholesterol; 7 g Carbohydrate; trace Fibre; 1 g Protein; 7 mg Sodium

white chocolate pecan cookies

Crisp cookies are the best for dunking into coffee or tea, and these definitely fit the bill.

Brown sugar, packed	3/4 cup	175 mL
Vanilla extract	1 tsp.	5 mL
Large egg	1	1
Pecans, toasted (see Tip, page 64) and coarsely chopped	1 1/2 cups	375 mL
White chocolate chips	1 cup	250 mL
All-purpose flour	3/4 cup	175 mL
Cooking oil	1/2 cup	125 mL
Medium unsweetened coconut	1/2 cup	125 mL
Baking powder	1/2 tsp.	2 mL
Ground cinnamon	1/4 tsp.	1 mL

Beat first 3 ingredients in medium bowl.

Add remaining 7 ingredients. Mix well. Chill, covered, for 30 minutes. Roll into balls, using about 1 tbsp. (15 mL) for each. Arrange on greased cookie sheets, about 2 inches (5 cm) apart. Bake in 350°F (175°C) oven for 12 to 15 minutes until edges are golden. Let stand on cookie sheets for 5 minutes before removing to wire racks to cool. Makes about 32 cookies.

1 cookie: 145 Calories; 10.4 g Total Fat (5.2 g Mono, 2.1 g Poly, 2.5 g Sat); 8 mg Cholesterol; 13 g Carbohydrate; 1 g Fibre; 1 g Protein; 16 mg Sodium

recipe index

topical tips

Canned pumpkin: Be careful to purchase the type of canned pumpkin that your recipe calls for. Pure pumpkin is just that—pumpkin with nothing added. Pumpkin pie filling, on the other hand, is pumpkin that has been blended with sugar and spices.

Peeling hazelnuts: Spread toasted nuts on half of a tea towel and fold the other half over the nuts. Press down and rub vigorously for 1 to 2 minutes, until almost all the skins are removed. You may not be able to remove all the skins from the hazelnuts, but the outer paper skins should come off.

Toasting nuts: When toasting nuts, seeds or coconut, cooking times will vary for each type of nut—so never toast them together. For small amounts, place the ingredient in an ungreased shallow frying pan. Heat on medium for 3 to 5 minutes, stirring often, until golden. For larger amounts, spread the ingredient evenly in an ungreased shallow pan. Bake in a 350°F (175°C) oven for 5 to 10 minutes, stirring or shaking often, until golden.

Nutrition Information Guidelines

Each recipe is analyzed using the Canadian Nutrient File from Health Canada, which is based on the United States Department of Agriculture (USDA) Nutrient Database.

- If more than one ingredient is listed (such as "butter or hard margarine"), or if a range is given (1–2 tsp., 5–10 mL), only the first ingredient or first amount is analyzed.

- For meat, poultry and fish, the serving size per person is based on the recommended 4 oz. (113 g) uncooked weight (without bone), which is 2–3 oz. (57–85 g) cooked weight (without bone)—approximately the size of a deck of playing cards.

- Milk used is 1% M.F. (milk fat), unless otherwise stated.

- Cooking oil used is canola oil, unless otherwise stated.

- Ingredients indicating "sprinkle," "optional" or "for garnish" are not included in the nutrition information.

- The fat in recipes and combination foods can vary greatly depending on the sources and types of fats used in each specific ingredient. For these reasons, the count of saturated, monounsaturated and polyunsaturated fats may not add up to the total fat content.